The Charm

The Charm

Poems by Kathy Fagan

Zoo Press

Zoo Press • P.O. Box 22990 • Lincoln, Nebraska 68542
Printed in the United States of America

Distributed to the trade by The University of Nebraska Press
Lincoln, Nebraska 68588 • www.nebraskapress.unl.edu

Cover design by Dana Frankfort © 2002

Fagan, Kathy.
  The charm / by Kathy Fagan.— 1st ed.
     p. cm.
  ISBN 0-9708177-4-6 (alk. paper)
  I. Title.
  PS3556.A326 C47 2002
  811'.54—dc21

zoo006

First Edition

Acknowledgments

Grateful acknowledgment is made to the editors of the journals and anthologies in which some of these poems originally appeared, sometimes in slightly different versions: *Central Ohio Writing*: selections from "Charm Bracelet"; *Connecticut Review*: "The Weather They Were Written In"; *Crab Orchard Review*: "Late Night Charm" (as "Late Night Ghazal"); *FIELD*: "Laine et Soie," "Charm for What Looks Like," and "Visitation"; *forpoetry.com*: "Little Bad Dream Charm"; *Gulf Coast*: "In California"; *Mid-American Review*: "Dancing with Adam"; *Nebraska Review*: "Other Voices, Many Forms"; *Ploughshares*: "Letter from the Garden"; *The Progressive*: "Tympani"; *San Joaquin Review*: "Little Bad Dream Charm"; *Sou'wester*: "Charm to Avoid Dying a Second Time"; *TriQuarterly*: "Aubergine Accords with Dove Charmingly," "Horsepower," and "Recovery."

"In California" also appeared in *The Geography of Home: California's Poetry of Place*, edited by Christopher Buckley and Gary Young, published by HeyDay Books in 1999. The poem is also reprinted in *American Diaspora: Poetry of Displacement*, edited by Virgil Suarez and Ryan G. Van Cleave, published by University of Iowa Press in 2001.

"The Weather They Were Written In" also appeared in *Pushcart Prizes XXIII*, edited by Bill Henderson, published by Pushcart Press in 1999. The poem is also reprinted in *The Breath of Parted Lips: Voices from the Robert Frost Place*, edited by Joan Cusack Handler, published by Cavan Kerry Press in 2001.

My thanks to the Ohio Arts Council for a grant which helped with the completion of this manuscript, and to The Ohio State University for time in which to work.

For Tom & Oscar,

    where there's always sun

  & for A,

    where there's always

Table of Contents

I

II

III

The leaden circles dissolved in the air...
                                    —Virginia Woolf

...and the charm of the carol rapt me.
                                    —Walt Whitman

I

Charm for What Looks Like

imaginary hats, real plastic
purses with chains

inside them, brown suit or sailor
depending on size, and rabbit

muffs molting on pastel
colors. Exactly one

beagle. A white house with rose
shutters too small to hold them

all, and a willow weeping
in the sideyard for the dead boy

day and night. What looks like
America in hats and gloves

is. With mother and father young
enough to be your own children, how

will you blame them now?
What looks like nostalgia

isn't. Nobody really wants to
relive it. We're all too tired

from turning the century. Is that where
your body was? Poor body,

having to get from there to here—
in those shoes! For some things

there are no photographs. A Friday
night in May, for example, when it's hard

to get a sitter. There are recipes for disaster
but you don't know them yet.

The moon lights the clouds and the clouds
race along the phone lines looking

like a train or
a story. Mother and father have

stepped out, how
can you blame them?

They have friends everywhere
in houses like yours, yellow

windows striped black with venetian blinds.
The phone off the hook in your kitchen

connects to the phone off the hook
where they are. You're supposed to be

in bed, but in the story you-never-slept-
a-wink-as-a-child, well, how

can they blame you?
In the receiver at your ear are

underwater voices, a chair scraped
back, something set down in your

head. Exactly once, twice, three
times you say hello into the mouthpiece in

whispers from low to medium to
loud. It would be a story if you cried out,

but it looks like you never cried
out. It would be a story if you hung up,

but, often as you pushed
on that phone's plastic nipples—

lightly lightly—heart
racing like a cloud at each click,

it looks like you
never hung up. Is it still a story

when nothing's happened yet?
When you stuff as many cookies in your mouth

as will fit and try on
your father's wingtips and your mother's best

strand of phony pearls and look like
someone so like you in the mirror

you could weep like a tree?
The only recipe you know by heart

is for homemade bubbles, which calls for water
and a cup of Joy.

Alas, My Heart, If I Could Bare / My Heart...

would be a bell,
hollow body with tongue
attached, not yet
pealing, everted
orifice, inverted
cup, not yet
pealing, but protecting
the tender: bella,
bellus, bellum,
protect them:
offertory, bluebell,
schoolbell, & the hand
to ring them,
pealing now,
wedding, vesper, &
dirge, pealing now,
to mark the time
& track the cat
from whom the finches
flee, bell
at her throat like
a flower's corona,
flare at the mouth of the wind
instrument, bellow
of the rutting
buck & bay of
the hound who hunts it:
bawl, blow, swell, & bubble—
take this cup from me
& make of it a bell enclosed—
like the silver sphere
I gave my friend,
its small music

rolling in her hand.
When she died
her parents locked it
in a china cabinet,
a light trained on it
like an egg.

Visitation

An hour before dusk on a Tuesday, mid-November—
sunstruck clouds with winter in them,
beeches, sycamores, white with it too.
Blue sky. Also
an aroma of blue
sky, bell-clear, hard as a river
in your lungs, which is why you're
breathless again, grateful,
as if it were the banks of the Seine
you strolled on and not
the mastodon back of the Midwest,
gray unraiseable thing like a childhood
slept through, and past.
On the horizon now a kind of golden
gate of sunset. To visit
means to both comfort and afflict,
though neither lasts long.
That charm of finches lifting from a ditch
can surprise you with a sound like
horselips, and paddle toward the trees
beautifully, small,
brown, forgettable as seeds,
but they, too, must sing on earth unto the bitter death—

Charm for an Unwritten Character

She'd be a woman with a lot of brothers,
a woman who wore charm bracelets.

On the one hand
she'd consider her childhood lucky:
She'd been deadly serious about boys,
believed God was a gentleman,
ate soft-boiled eggs from a cup,
liked the salt best.

To this day
she'd be willing to sit in an exit row,
type 65 wpm,
eat her soup, speak her mind, walk this way.

On the other hand
she'd abhor the housecoat,
the piebald horse's big horse face,
its tail the color of her hair in spots.
She'd believe in things more than mercy,
in facts:

When Elvis Presley died in 1977, for example,
there were 48 professional Elvis impersonators.
In 1996, there were 7,328.
If this rate of growth continues, by the year 2012,
one person in every four will be an Elvis impersonator.

She doesn't want to live to see the day.
She wants to live to see the day.

She'd be a woman with a lot of sons,
and one daughter, whose name continually changes.

She'd believe in duty and the life of the mind,
in memorization and recitation:

> *And again sighing she spoke:"A dream*
> *That once was mine! what woman taught you this?"*

Earliest Memory:
9/1/14: Martha,
the last passenger pigeon,
dies at the Cincinnati Zoo.

Or:
Lilacs,
purple lilacs on a long white field,
and scalloped curtains at the window breathing.

Most Extravagant Shopping Spree:
Frederick Cooper's Lamps of Elegance, Chicago, 1952.

Favorite Travel Destination:
The Café In Person.

Favorite Article of Clothing:
His coat.

Favorite Phrases:
Mother of God!
Do as you please.
Where are my good shoes?

Least Favorite:
The phrase "prior to."
The phrase "I'd like to thank."
The word "flow."
The question "Do you think the poet intended that?"
The answer "Yes and no. That and more."

Great Poets Steal

and you get used
to it: the occasional stuffing of a rhyme
down a blouse, the anecdote
up a sleeve, the sort of communal
metaphor that sticks
to their facial hairs—
but she's a bon mot klepto of
felonious proportions, passing
up the drinks and canapés, the chance
to bounce your cute new baby, strictly
for conversation, a little one-
sided tête-à-tête-à-
tête, like she's burning
CDs of them, penning the highlights in
to her palm—
not that you're some genius,
but she will be,
in several languages,
copyrighted, film-optioned: read it
and weep—and say what
you will, face it,
she will too,
because she's a bon mot klepto
who's robbing you speechless,
she's slipping security, jumping the stile—
and there's nothing left
to say, of course, because she's taken
the right word right out of
your mouth—
and it glints like
a gun when she grins: goodbye.

Misfortune Cookies

Expect a run of good luck
in Gary, Indiana.

Your abundant gifts will be rewarded
by a local philatelic organization.

Your cat often has bad hair days and curses at life.

You possess an unrequited love of language.

We all fall down a rabbit hole
but that doesn't mean we all get tea afterward
or good advice.

What would you do with a pomegranate if you had one?

You are passionate and hirsute.

Without briefs, how will you plead your firm case?

Creative people are attracted to you
because of the metal plate in your head.

Your dermatitis makes you a popular party guest.

You piss people off but they can't say why.

Stick to your current path and you will find
pant suits at discount prices.

A little personality would do you good.

It is a well-established but widely under-reported phenomenon
that molecules in women over 40 destabilize,
often rendering them invisible to the naked eye.
In fact, all your dinner companion sees now
as he looks across the table
is a large fortune cookie cracked open in your place.

Never shout fire. Always stay calm.

Everything will fall into place in the days to come.

The sledding hill will remain closed.

Those born prior to 1972 will not be permitted to purchase
the Jimi Hendrix T-shirts.

That boy they call Chud will be famous one day,
so you should get an autograph and maybe a pair of his socks
while you still can.

Measure twice, marry once.

Look ahead.

Watch your back.

Chin up.

Stomach in.

Straighten out.

Blend well, not ignoring the hairline.

Shut up and repeat this to no one.

Invective

I am mad at the houses,
each with its own roof and the same
stupid trees.

I hate all the lawns,
that only look good
for maybe eight minutes on a Thursday in June
some leap years.

And the people who sew,
and their blah blah blah all the time about
selvage and interfacing.

And the golfers with their bunkers and roughs,
like it was a war they waged—in plaid,
in a park. I mean, what they do in private is their business,
but I don't need it shoved in my face.

Wall-to-wall carpet really pisses me off.
Who thought of it? Let's kill him.

Let's burn the catalogues,
ban barcodes,
SUVs, minivans, especially
green ones.

Let's punish employees who spray Lysol on neighboring tables
when you're trying to eat your ice cream.

And the kid behind me on the plane, flying for the first time—
I swear, when we're above the clouds and he says how this must be
        heaven,
I want to clock him.

Like Courtney Love, I've begun to believe that chicken is truly evil.
We shouldn't eat it. Eat it and I'll hate you. I really will.

Because the great thing about anger
is how it multiplies.

On the other hand,
the trouble with anger—

I almost wrote *The Trouble with Angels*,
a movie classic from the 60s featuring angry nuns on a bus,
Hayley Mills as a student, who is always angry,
and Rosalind Russell as Mother Superior, who also made a career
            of being angry,
and large-breasted—

the trouble with anger,
as my friend Dolores told me before she died,
is that it's really only fear disguised.

But she's dead, is how much she knew about it.

I was buying a tasty low-salt cracker at the health food store for
            the longest time
and now they don't carry it anymore.
I can't tell you how mad that makes me,
can I?

Charm for Max Ernst

after his painting "2 Children are Threatened by a Nightingale"

Someone's been hit.
Somebody's down like an anchovy in the running
in the meanwhile melee.

And though the gate gapes red on its hinges
and the lever's been thrown to alarum on the firebox, no one
is coming, no one will

come. Mother must brandish her weapon alone—
bust pointed forward, hair bolted back,
she's a shape of cold water where her body was—

while father goalruns their girl away,
a nacreous comma in his chromey grip, a sleeping
supple, roof-vaulting lightly...

He's a bluespool hero
in his weathervane posturing if ever there was
a lightning rod.

Night terrors. Child's play.
The one true faith was always fear,
hortus conclusus with no garden in it,

each lawn a choppy ocean
and a renaissance sky out every window, the usual
history creeping in.

Will the little fish recover?
Will mother ever wield the knife enough to suit her?
Will father reinvent the wheel in time?

No matter.

Now sun spreads like lemon cream from the east,
and on its stain ride
smoky India, archy France.

And nightingale, like any good vampire,
has had its fill of blood for one night.
O, for a draught of that vintage!

Come, let us close the gate again.
We'd only wanted to scare them a little.

Horsepower

The point being a line
but not a straight line

Motion   Fragment   Track   &   Clatter

That train has 4 engines she said
This train 2

Never before had I considered the equation

Each car looked too dry & empty

In the desert one sees them set up on blocks
the color of old blood or bananas

For chickens maybe
the family
dog

A child of my century I just kept thinking
Death Camps
the trains to

Head on they were beautiful in the olden days
What wasn't

They're eel-faced now the passenger kind with the names of Vegas casinos

The eel could have come from a nightmare of mine
(Nightmare   Horsepower)

Or from the magnified photo of a spirochete
My hand recoiling like it was a wet rock I'd turned over & not
a page not
a simple picture on a simple page

The point being there are other
trains of thought
assemblies of them
assemblages

Spirochete   Parakeet   Paraclete
Some species are known to mimic human speech

Stout bills both
the finch is from another family altogether so never does

They court on electrical wires instead
bodies accommodating for the bob
their heads stained red for having relieved the savior of his scourge
          of thorns

Males were rewarded for that with the color of his blood
Females on the other hand
a soft brown all over
look horned while they're mating from where they're peaked &
          bitten

There are only so many
flying things
Even fewer swim

Train of thought   School of fish

When my friend's dead koi came back to life she named them Jesus
I II & III
Jesus cubed
The Last Supper

The point being the truth
is never simple

Or rarely
rarely is it

(Look said the child pointing to her bathwater
Look she said
Pink fishes)

It could just as easily be
hooved

Charm for Joseph Cornell

CHARACTERS

CHILDHOOD, *a memory*
SOLITUDE, *his brother*
FAMOUS BEAUTY, *herself*

SCENE: Interior

ACT 5, Scene 1
Snow in the quince tree. A flutter of wings.

CHILDHOOD: Does it have
an Alp,
an Owl,
a Star?

SOLITUDE: There are so many
somethings,
so much varied weather
in one's head,

BEAUTY: air in the proscenium.

& in the transparent
envelope,
one word:
TINSEL

Exeunt omnes.

II

Aubergine Accords with Dove Charmingly.

Daily Chronicle, *21 November 1903*

In fact, all accords with dove when dove has its way—
the hinge-winged peacenik, the alpha and omega pairs of them.
What Aphrodite and Jonah have in common is the dove,
as do all the twos on Noah's Ark, and the seven rings round
the oft-rung throat, which is the Holy Spirit's ROY G. BIV
buckling and glinting, racing the scales with each regurgitation.
Rys vp my wyf, my loue, my lady free, my dowue sweete.
Close to the hinder feet of Canis Major they snag a supper
and settle down to brood on a few of their olive branches.
The male brings up his crop milk for the squabs (insert
diacritical beak here); all breast, they're sheer
fuselage, Pontormo-painted, their poop, prodigious.
What they fly for is the roosting place.
My heart, but you were dovewinged, I can tell.
By which the poet, writing of the wreck, must have meant
the shuddering whistle of the wings in flight.
For in repose, they make a different noise.

Dancing with Adam

Adam is inconsolable.
He is wailing his grief
word: *Chu-a-lar.*
He is trying it out like a key,
like the secret name of his truest home,
yodeling it
until I want back too.

And who shall deliver us
Chualar
unto Krypton, Israel, Avalon, Narnia?
Our parents, asleep then,
are sleeping still. O
faithful Adam, forsaken boy,
let us dance for comfort *Chualar,*
let me sing you the tail ends of the soft
songs for accompaniment.

For just as sure as spring will bring
Spin
all the words that love can sing
Spangle
I will be remembering
the shadow of your shadow
when the crying stops.

And when we dip
where the horns would be after
Tell Me You'll Love Me
For a Million Years, you do
almost smile,
as you did that night,
learning *Happy New Year,*
happy, happy—
Ps plosive as a comic drunk's.

In an old dream I sang and danced like this
defying Death,
my unconscious a regular Bergman.
In the new
I speak a word that's true and am forgiven.
I am always wishing to
get back into that dream again,

like a news dispenser when the lid falls shut—
for a quarter you can take as many as you like,
but then what?
The headline reads
Tiger, Lion Taken from Homeless Man,
and the man in the story is pleading
Chualar
These cats are my life.
These cats are my children.

Boys track by on their boards and blades,
tremors at a time of them, slamming
the coin returns,
doing the job too fast,
something pulling them,
feet forward,
like metal shavings.

The story says that for years he's kept them
in the 10 x 7 x 7 foot
cage of a converted delivery truck,
that both animals appear well cared for,
that Aslan is his favorite.
He was yours.
I am always wishing
to get into that dream again,
to hold

open its magic name,
its lovely
meaning:
Jesus, Spring,
a million happy,
happy new....
Aslan is everyone's favorite.

Laine et Soie

Name the animals that guard him.
    Monkey, lion, stag, porcupine, unicorn.
Any other?
    A nightingale in the foliage,
    her breast torn with song.
How do they guard him?
    Like numerals on a green clock.
And Stephen's body?
    The hands of that clock
    at 9:15.
From whom does he need protection?
    Now, only from idle aristocrats.
And the angels?
    Two, to escort him.
    Their wings are like blades.
Like the unicorn's tusk.
    And the porcupine's quills, and the nimbed rays
    round the saint's head
    that the lion tastes with the tip of his tongue.
All that pointing!
    And more: stag rack, castle tower,
    the leafy sharpness of holly, oak,
    and the thorn on the...
Rose.
    I was going to say *nightingale.*
    The thorn in the nightingale's...
Standing for?
    Christ.
Standing for?
    Christ.
And?
    The weavers, their
    needles, their
    fingers stained madder and woad.

Tympani

Pomegranate beads loose
bracelets of them & under the skins
the small pink juices
a weight that drums as it falls to the table

Not the kettledrums of telethons drummed up drummed
out but tympani nonetheless

Like the difference between the Woolworth Building &
the 5&10 my grandparents ate breakfast in
sopping their tea up the Irish way
the way the word
martyr carries its own cross and the garter
snake wears them but whose leg not his
the way the offertory bells lifted
like the lid off a platter lamb
of god fisher of men prince of peace doorbell & phone
rung & the way we pretended Hello, Jesus?

Bells & drums lights & whistles
Blow flash & blossom

In 1906 the owners of Luna Park
decided Coney Island's electrical plant could do more
than light an amusement park and successfully
electrocuted one of their herd of working elephants.
It took ten seconds.
In silent footage Topsy is alive,
then a long stillness,
then the crumpling mass of her body,

& after
& after that

glitter tremble

Here are the seeds
they are ripe to bursting
they are ripe to bursting the drums of their bodies
this is my body
tympani toteboard reprise &
the hour chiming
& then the curtain (deus) rises—
or does it part

Kind Delicatessen

Nightmares can't find me here.

Solace is
its own metaphor, its aspirin
a bitter moon to chew.
The sentence can croon again
its fine and lit effects,
but were words set down—shattered, broken—
ever so ever so loose a thing and dying?

I have a handsome gentleman
with ten words
dedicated
to the working classes:

Hunger
        Swan
                Train
and
                        Backbone.

His damn underage floozies
with their verses wideflung
(hunched over waffles no verse is wideflung),
who among them can bear to feel?
Who can stand what the meal has cost them?
Each and every word is common.

I am not assigned the nightshift
Sundays much.
The others—missing, sick—
have left
mittened Worry to help us.
It's not been my assistant.

Shall we
whine and give thanks and get fat again?
have children in nine midwestern states?
order rum? order gin?
Does what happens interest God?
force the Libido into voice?
meddle in her words, her unsure consonants?

Maybe.
With them: art, ten haggling cops.
With them: writer's cramp in both hands,
thunder, dry thunder, and night again, as they say, dropped.
I am ripping this paper
wide open, the angry wide open
operatic voice. Do our mothers see us?

We are here.

O dark, sullen andirons.

I am tired. It is so forlorn here.

Letter from the Garden

Three days of spring winter and suddenly,
birds everywhere. The sky and garden
are not enough for them. They beat upon
the pane of glass through which I watch them, wanting
entrance. It was wrong to think that they
were happier than I, or that nothing
was denied them, when I, myself, had shut
them out. My love, paradise is lonely
for you; and your dream of redemption, but
a fleshly longing that makes my life even
lonelier still. There's a place for you here
at the teeming window, where I promise,
I will not touch you again, or punish us further
with any desire, any desire but this.

Late Night Charm

Life, you say, is like TV.
How small we are. How shiny,

with somebody always the skipper,
someone else, his little buddy.

I'm thinking Ginger, Maryann—
but you're drifting off by

now, your teeth showing like Flipper's
when he's happy.

Was Doris Day in "The Glass Bottom
Boat"? How many

times have you seen "Mr. Limpet"?
Did you ever see

"Dear Brigitte," where the little boy,
who's the son of Jimmy

Stewart, is writing love letters
to Brigitte Bardot in France? He's

in love with her, even though
he's, like, eight. He doesn't see

the problem. He's conjugating French verbs.
He wants to fly to Paris. The family

can't afford that, of course
(I think poor Jimmy

is a college professor), and they're
having their vacation already

anyhow, on a boat, which I guess
is why I thought of it. You're sound asleep.

Why do they call it sound
asleep? I hit the mute. It makes me

lonely. It makes me feel more free
to talk. Bardot is only

in it for a minute. Did you ever want to
sleep with her? You look so tiny

in this gray light. Slick, silvery, loyal.
Why that makes me lonely stumps me.

I turn the sound back on. You stir a bit.
Hush, I say. Hush, *mon petit.*

Mon petit dauphin. Mon petit anchois.
It's only me. Go back to sleep.

Little Bad Dream Charm

We haven't found enough dreams. We haven't dreamed enough.
—Georgia O'Keeffe

I just work up from a start afternoon nap. I
dreamed of whole time. I dreamed I woke up
lists of times. I wanted to make up, because
all my drears were nightmares. The only reason
I thank I'm awake now is that I'm steel sleepy.
I dreamed about goldfish except they were boys,
and there were hundreds of ether boys, some
so tinny they were trapped in the weave of a green
carpet that shone like water or glass—sea, that's
why it was a bad dream. They were all dying
because they were leafing out of their tanks. I
had scooped them up and threw them back into any
whaler I could find—I had stuffed, even, two
plastic caps full. And then, in order to save
as many lines as I could, I scooped a whole
bunch into an aquarium, awe at once—and that's
what they became soddenly, enormous carrots
sinking to the bittern of the dark.

Charm to Avoid Dying a Second Time

In the Egyptian Book of The Dead, just at the point where the soul can enter
Paradise and live forever, there are words the dead traveler must recite

In order to avoid dying a second time. To a 21st century westerner, dying
A second time might sound like a deal, loving second chances as we do,

Our faith founded firmly on practice and rehearsal. After the first time, for
        example,
You'd know to say something more memorable on your deathbed, or be savvier

About the will. But for the ancient Egyptians, dying was worse than death,
With all the low points of actually dying, plus the hassle of mummification,

Getting your wives and servants sacrificed, moving a good chunk of the household
Into the cramped quarters of the tomb. Then there's the reading, great walls

Of impenetrable text. Don't do the reading, don't pass the tests; don't pass
The tests, don't have an afterlife—sort of like the GRE. And with gods

Like the jackal-headed Thoth barking at you to hand over your soul—*If you plan
On repelling serpents and avoiding worms, you'll get your soul weighed and get it*

Weighed now!—you could get the impression that an afterlife is simply not
Worth having, though you'd have to admit, the makeup and jewelry are fabulous.

Truth is, only the wealthy worked this hard in death, had the leisure and means
To control both lives and afterlives—or so they thought. The rest, perhaps,

Were more like us. The dead mostly get tired and die, and the living, believers
Or not, wonder where they go, and would, god help them, bring the dead

Back, tired or not, because this is the best place for us, body and soul, to die
A little more every day.

Charm to Allay the Primitive Fear of Having to Walk Upside Down

Which is perhaps the one phobia that does not afflict anyone I know personally
And which can probably be explained by an Egyptian aversion to underwear

As we now know it and the fact that pants of any kind had not yet been invented.
Fred Astaire defied the gods by dancing upside down, but Fred Astaire

Was wearing pants, and neither Egyptian nor dead, at that time.
Come to think of it, having to walk on your hands could be what

The ancient Egyptians feared most. It would be hell, really, even for an acrobat,
Requiring a steady supply of sturdy utility gloves, and frequent rest periods—

Though it might be great from your dog's point of view, and could lead
To pretty phenomenal bench press averages. Who says we should be walking

Right side up anyway? Babies look like they could go either way, early on,
And a friend in a wheel chair thinks walking upside down might be a nice change

Of pace. Any kind of conformity, after all, can be a life sentence. Sisyphus
And the guy tied to the rock getting his liver pecked out for eternity: At some point

They had to say, *Oh, please, are we still doing this?* In fact the only advantage
I can see in walking the way we do now, besides the compulsive shoe shopping,

Is that nobody notices, and in some things a person doesn't want to stand out.
Actually, the most primitive fear of all might be the fear of being different,

And after a lifetime of feeling alienated in a thousand ways, one might think it
A just reward to belong utterly, to walk upright among the smugly dead

And feel smug oneself, feet for once planted firmly on the ground, head held high.
If somewhere's too far to walk, you take your SUV, because there's no mass transit,

And everyone's hands are clean.

III

In California

one either believes in God
or believes one is
God. Like the freeway, you can't drive on
both sides at once.
Medians themselves are horticultural
phenomena. And from every direction there is
vista, there is grande.
There are places called
Vista Grande.
I have seen them myself,
have the photos to prove it.
I have stepped from my car in a glockenspiel
shirtfront and conducted
orchestras.
I have held in my hand a baton of sky,
while the hills looped gold
green   silver   black,
and the automatic tollbooths rang and rang,
lifting and letting fall
their braceleted arms.

In California there is more
land than ocean; we will not
discuss then, in this poem, the ocean.
Let us place coins where its eyes used to be
and insist instead,
as wisteria insists—
the insistent part of the wisteria—on
architecture. Consider
the bungalow, the overpass, the balcony
balustrade as muscular as any Mister
Atlas, tiny kites wound
round his triceps. And the palms:

it's not just headdresses with them
but mufflers, full-length
raccoon coats, that trailing
perfume of fennel and sage, a dust
that will not dust
off. Not off the palm, not off the grape,
not off the live oak or
the dead. Rolling the piers and streets and orchards,
only the fog can slick it down.

I take it back
about the kites. I see now the five points,
the pentagons of morning
glory choking the balcony,
and potted nasturtiums on the landing
gleaming. How our grandmothers favored them,
the old flowers, old edible
flowers. Like the old
stories, they have it all:
feet of clay, suits of mail,
coats of brine, hoops of gold....

Red Aster, who made you?
The Sun made me.
And who, Red Aster, ringed you with gold?
You have, Maestro, who planted me here.

China

We were always digging for it in those days—
with spoons. Then we forgot it, for decades

until today, digging in a backyard
that yields only weeds, tomatoes and basil

if we nurse them, and one perfect marble,
it seems, each spring. But this must be

what they really meant when they said,
You'll dig all the way to: this inch of

children's china, this third of a nimbus of
broken saucer, white in my muddy glove,

but for two crudely drawn—would they be
daisies, or stars, clay-colored, or spice-?

You choose. There's one for each of us.

Recovery

Remember. Resurrect. A river
Taken under the rain's
    Right arm. Enter an R and everything rises,
Like cream, to the surface.

    It's the ornamental nature of the peacock
Letter. From its azure
    Crest to its emerald
Throat to the Roman grandeur of its mirrored

    Train—iridescence runneth over!
Red rover, red rover. And look! *Regarde!*
    Our laureates rush over—
To write us a rhyme, a romance, or retraction,

    To write an Rx for our grieving
Hearts: *Turn words every morning like a bride*
    In your arms and repeat after me:
Resh. Ra. Roar. Rabbi. I am

    Wronged. I am wrong. Dark.
Sorrow. Rare. Miracle. Adorable. Reaper. Raison
    D'etre. We are
Irreparable. But what of it?

    Therefore shall we labor
In the service of the R.
    Therefore shall we practice
Such random acts of artifice as

    The topiary, curlicue of orange
Rind, and other ethereal arrangements of the sort
    Featured in Martha Stewart's
Marathon pre-Christmas broadcast,

"An Undecorated Life Is Not Worth Living."
Pre-recorded in the recently renovated
     Rooms of her rustic 18th century Vermont,
Paris, Prague, and Ozark farmhouses,

     She credits Ezra Pound and his celebrated Modern
Maxim, "Make It New,"
     For her own mantra: "Make It Yourself,
Make It Pretty, and Keep the Glue-gun Loaded."

     Despair prepared for is despair
Averted. The R knows that. As do charm,
     Conjury, and all rarefied matters of inconsequence
I was formerly

     Forever railing against. No longer.

Charm Bracelet

Kitchen Haiku

Kitchen remodel:
it's hell on a manicure.
Backyard squirrels don't care.

*

Kitchen remodel:
no sex on this formica—
what day's the floor laid?

*

Kitchen remodel:
arctic mélange, maple plank,
seed pearl and *mission.*

EBAY Haiku with Occasional Tanka

Can you trust a thing
with No Reserve, a site that
welcomes New Users?

*

Item condition:
No chips or cracks, some crazing,
NICE!—like my mother.

*

This is a old piece.
She has a face problem green
body. Hair is a
orange color. She is numb-
ered on the bottom of her.

*

There is one other
issue, the tip of the top
of the sky is chipped
otherwise in Very Good
Condition. Happy Bidding!!!

Childless Haiku with Concluding Tanka

Spring, and everything
knocked up but me. I should be
as thin as winter.

*

It's a Xerox world.
Bare butts on the copier.
Babies all over.

*

Since these won't get born,
I name them with abandon:
Harry, Louis, Moe.

*

Our parents' favorite
curse then was: Hope you have kids
bad as you kids are.
And sometimes I think I hear
mine, breaking her mother's heart.

'50s Poets Haiku with Opening Tanka

In pictures Lowell looks
like someone playing Jesus,
which is what Jesus
always looks like: self-consciously,
regrettably well-bred.

*

The Norton says Plath,
all saddle shoes and report cards,
made much of little.

Her final success,
the Norton says, was sticking
her head in an oven.

         *

Delmore talked, drunk or
sober, tongues of fire; named his
kitten *Oranges*.

         *

Bishop wished they'd kept
some things to themselves. Turns out
she couldn't either.

         *

In his haiku Auden counted
words not syllables, thereby avoiding lines like
W. H. Au—.

Literary Prize Haiku

I want the French one:
Prix Femina Etranger,
the strange woman prize—

and I should have it,
mais, tant pis pour moi, I'll have
to write a novel

first. That's a lot of
haiku. Must I die proving
poets are stranger?

Fall to Summer Haiku

Oak leaves, school shoes, brick
brick brick. Ordinary Bronx
autumn, Vermeer browns.

*

Snow outside. Beneath
me, floorboards sun has found. What
gold from the toes up!

*

Because all things die
my sweetie says no to spring.
Plants grow anyway.

*

Jets glint like razors
in the June sky. How quickly
we leave each other.

In the Museum of Not Real History

the US drinks Canada Dry & we are all 2 Good 2 B
4 Gotten (museum curators graduated circa 1958).
In the Museum of Not Real History, lullaby
ends, as I always suspected it should, with an E,

& in the index to Wallace Stevens's *Collected*
Poems, there are titles beginning with K, X, & Z.
In the Museum of Not Real History, all children
are liars & I have nine of them, hovering like

stars around my head as I make my ascension
into heaven (or is it the West Side Y?). For I
am their tree, their truth, their beech, & their
book, & they are my nestlings, needing oiling—

such rusty apparatuses, those mouths & wings,
spasming wetly! In the Museum of Not Real History,
the walls are white, without a nail hole or speck
of blood. There is no spectacle of any kind,

nor is there debacle, canticle, cubicle, or fascicle,
nor need of the F-word except in pleasure.
Rooms are large; CDs have yet to be invented;
museum guards play LPs & drive small cars

to work instead, mostly VWs. Because, remember,
this is the Museum of Not Real History, where N-O
means no & everyone minds their Ps & Qs. LBJ
never became president & there's still a G

in the word baloney—reminding me suddenly that
the technology for the MRI does not exist, which is
too bad because I haven't been feeling well since
taking that spill down the museum stairs. It was

as I lay there, prone on the marble, gazing up
at the museum's reproduction of T-Rex, nine stars
circling round my head, that it dawned on me
what a tyrant history is, real or not, always

plopping us somewhere on its continuum & telling us
to stay like the good alphabets we are, telling us
to say AH, say please, say thank you, say good night
Gracie. After the MUSE in museum, we're left with UM.

Picasso's Toenails

Where, now, are the toenail clippings of Picasso, preserved by Picasso's
Wife? She pared them herself with a kitchen knife, just as Picasso

Asked her to, though some nails were jagged as a horse's tongue,
And some curled shyly under, round as the breasts on Picasso's

Nudes. There were blue ones and rose ones, and some Picasso called his doves
As they fluttered to the floor, forming Xs and Os, like Paloma Picasso's

Signature earrings. The father's love is an immortal love,
With DNA in it. I should know. Picasso

Loves me like his own creation. *KAT-D*, he calls me, even in letters. *My
        dear KAT-D,
Of pleasure and proof, only proof endures. I miss pleasure more. Yr Picasso.*

Charms from an English Grammar

190. Verbs, Transitive and Intransitive.

He wished to live. They tried to run. She commenced to work. They professed to find gold. I want what will be useful. Men love to be flattered. I know that you will try to be upright. You say that he is honest. I know who did it. I heard what was said. Govern your passions, and you will escape many troubles. He believes that the earth is round. What do you say? Whom did you see? The question which you ask I cannot answer. John told what he knew to be false. Thee we adore, Supreme Ruler! When did he go? He was a scholar and an author. The moon rose above the trees. The hills looked blue in the distance. Our friends have come. Will you be present? James wrote to his father, and described his journey. I am not responsible for what he says.

Rule XV.—Prepositions.

I have a friend on whom I cannot rely. He is engaged in a great work. I find great difficulty in writing. Every change is not a change for the better. Virtue and vice differ widely from each other. What if the boy falls into a deep pit? Our principles cannot be reconciled to our practice. I have profited by his advice. I pass through the room. Crossing the Alps is attended by many difficulties. Hannibal forced his way into Italy. We have great abhorrence to such conduct, but I have little influence over him. He was accused of having acted unfairly. Few men can rise above popular prejudices. He eventually died of thirst. He was always aspiring to distinction, but never arrived at it. He tore the paper into pieces.

Rule XVI.—Conjunctions and Correlatives.

Correct the errors in the following examples.

Neither despise or oppose what you do not understand. There is no condition so secure as it may not admit of change. He does not converse with such who cannot bear contradiction. It shall not be forgiven him in this world, neither in the world to come. I would rather go as stay. I have no other hope but this. What else did he expect but disgrace? I would rather spend my time reading as working. This is none other but the gate of Paradise. Have you no other books except these? He no sooner sees her, but he runs to embrace her. The reward has already, or will hereafter be given to him. Teaching always has, and always will be laudable. London is larger, but not so fine a city as Paris. The camel has as much strength, and more endurance than the horse. His intentions might have and perhaps were good. I have, and still pretend to be a judge of these matters. In candid minds, truth finds an entrance, and a welcome too.

266. Remarks on Verbs.

2. The perfect participle must not be used for the past tense.

They did the best they could. He ran all the way. He began to write. I never saw it. They came in late yesterday. He drank at the fountain of knowledge. I saw him when he did it. He afterwards became a good scholar, and soon began to weary of being idle.

4. That which is always true should be expressed by the present tense.

Correct by Remark 4.

His master taught him that happiness consisted in virtue. Our teacher told us that the air had weight. Plato maintained that God was the soul of the universe. The philosopher said that heat expanded metals. He said that truth was immutable. Copernicus believed that the sun was the center of the solar system. He asserted that England was as free as any country on the globe. I have already told you that I was a gentleman. Heat will radiate best from rough substances. Kane believed that there was an open polar sea at the North Pole. He claimed that woman has a right to think and act for herself. I should never have discovered that this was poetry. The teacher explained to the pupils that the earth was a sphere. There are those who made a shipwreck of their faith.

9. An intransitive verb should not have the passive form; as, They have *fled; not, They* are *fled.* *

The tumult has entirely ceased. What has become of your brother? I have not come to take you away from your friends. My friends have all forsaken me. The heathen have perished out of the land. Only I have escaped to tell thee. When they came, they found that the empress had departed. He had retired to his tent. Claudius was vexed, because his wife had become a Christian. We have agreed on this. If you are injured, if you have injured, what has become of the injury?

* This expression is sometimes used by good writers; but it is contrary to the principles of the language.

August

Because when rain falls finally
everything strains either into it or away.
Nestlings sway with their well-mouths
open and trees say *Talk to the hand,*
flipping their leaves up. Because when
the rain falls finally it hurts them a little,
like touch after none, like the moment
you know will not last that does last,
and lasts and lasts and lasts and then—
when exactly did he grow so thin
and why and who decided? Because
when rain falls finally the pond
must give up its silver, the windshield
its flash, and the black swan's orange
bill become the only value in the dark.
You glide by. It glides by. People are
sadder or less sad, depending.
Bougainvillea petals heap at curbsides.
And the whole world, which will never again be
without him, tilts south a little.
Why shouldn't it?

The Weather They Were Written In

To start somewhere:
the window, ice, what fire
formed reformed
in frost, and frost itself
an other thing
more private somehow, and
complex, pinioned
like birds' underwings—
an arc and drift
of darkly plumaged peaks.
       In one pane, there's
       a kind of lake lain in
       among them, beveled,
       small, but mostly clear,
       a peephole meant
       to see the cold through—weather
       that would surely
       liquefy your vision
       were you in it,
       weep things off to left
and right. But you
are not—out in it—
nor are you teary,
despite a robin, mirrored
in the glass,
who hurls his body at
his body, breathless
after each attempt.
He loves himself,
almost, to death, and who
       can blame him? His eyes
       are lovely, his barrel
       chest...! Look:
       the logic of the male
       cardinal

in snow is red that makes
the white bearable;
a chickadee's dressed
in birch tree's clothing;
and sparrow—little splinter,
little ash,
little antic where-
am-I—is little
but fat; she is too fat
in fact to fly,
and the sky is, anyhow,
too sharp
to fly through. Settle down
and think now. Didn't
Stevens write, of summer,
how what's solid
seems to vaporize,
denying form
or definition? And since
this is the opposite
of August, couldn't
smoke in winter prove
the converse may be
true? At least, a crow
has found a pillar
of it—stalled above
a chimney flue—
sure enough to huddle
near: a something
other, separate from,
by which to judge
and warm himself—a staggered
column, woodstove
smoke, that would be nothing
without its circumstance,
the small flesh
that needs it.

Other Voices, Many Forms

The world is hammered into shape this morning—
a world, *some* shapes, one
singular morning, unlike another.
Neighbors to the south are constructing a sundeck;
neighbors to the north get their gutters replaced.
Between them they'll soon have the seasons covered,
and the more human weathers of pleasure and fear.
Meanwhile the hammer, the saw, and the drill
have laid down a form with their metal
voices—as the violin played across the street
by someone I have never seen
creates a form,
and as rain that fills, states west of the music,
rivers refusing to be contained
is form of sorts,
a new idea. I had been thinking of
touch-up paint, of whitewashing over the sad
spots of lumber
bloomed on the massive trim of my room
when, in spite of the din and misery elsewhere,
Pure Grief dropped in—with her string of attendants—saying:
This house too was someone's idea;
and when I failed to understand:
You may rock your fretful heart in your hands
but never will it utter its realest name.
And then perhaps because of the whorl,
a honey I imagined in the fashioned wood,
I saw an angel
run from a bee
in the gilt-framed flutter of autumn noonlight.
And the bee's idea, if you could call it
"idea," his instinct or need
is pursuit of the girl

(for she *is* a child, in a costume of childhood).
He has outlasted summer
and is drunk on the memory,
on her gold wings and hair that look
like pollen, and the scent of her
throat like a flowering weed.
And the child's idea is simple
escape, which makes her look more
like an angel in earnest: hair, wings, white
drapery streaming, her will
as strong as her belief in Jesus
(though the bee's will too is a vibrating thing).
So where is her harness? the pulleys and cable?
Oh where the sugar to please him best?
Only one thing is certain
as the buzz-saw snags, on curling notes,
and starts again against the press:
the neighborhood can't shut up today.
And no one pauses
as they might in a poem.
No one stops their work to listen.
There's a voice on the right climbing
rungs on a ladder; it mutters
to itself as I write this now:
Damn, just once, then *Damn* again,
Damn that damned violin music.

Notes

"Alas, My Heart, If I Could Bare/ My Heart...": Christina Rossetti's "Goblin Market."

"Visitation": "O, God...Thou art well acquainted with meals of thorns; yet Thou too hast sung on earth unto the bitter death." Conrad Von Megenberg's *Buch der Natur.*

"Charm for an Unwritten Character": Alfred Lord Tennyson's "The Princess."

"Misfortune Cookies" is for my students.

"Charm for Max Ernst": John Keats's "Ode to a Nightingale."

"Horsepower" is for Fritha S. Davern.

"Aubergine Accords with Dove Charmingly.": Geoffrey Chaucer's "The Merchant's Tale" and Gerard Manley Hopkins's "Wreck of the Deutschland."

"Dancing with Adam" is for Adam Cumurcu.

"Laine et Soie": Based on the St Etienne tapestry, circa 1500, Brussels, housed now in the Cluny Museum.

"Kind Delicatessen": Influenced by Ingeborg Bachmann's poem "Keine Delikatessen" ("No Delicacies").

"In the Museum of Not Real History" is for Grace Jane Herman Holland.

"Charms from an English Grammar": Andrew Burtt's *A Practical Grammar of the English Language, Synthetic and Analytic,* 1873.